DIL AAJ SHAYAR HAI

Confessions of a Bipolar Mind in Verse

By Rizwan Siddiqui
Published: 2025

Dedication

To those who struggle to come out of their misery, those
who are waiting for someone to come and rescue them.
To the ones who still have life left in them.

Acknowledgments

I would like to express my deepest gratitude to those who have supported me through this journey. Your encouragement, belief, and love have given me the strength to put my thoughts into words.

A special thanks to my son, you are the reason I write. This book belongs as much to you as it does to me.

Introduction

I did not write this book for validation. I do not write for comfort.
 I write because my mind is a battlefield. It runs so fast that by the time I am midway through my thoughts, my entire body is exhausted. If I don't let these words out, they will turn against me.

So read this not as poetry, but as evidence.
 Evidence that I was here.
 Evidence that I tried and failed most of the time but failed legendarily.
 Evidence that I felt everything too deeply.
 That I questioned, that I cursed, that I broke and rebuilt myself a hundred times over.

There is no healing in these pages. No final resolution.
 Just a man still figuring out whether his suffering is self-inflicted or inherited.

If you find a part of yourself in these words, don't look for hope. Just know that you are not alone in your restless-ness. And maybe just maybe that will be enough.

Rizwan

Why I wrote this poem

I thought *manzil* would feel like a reward.
But every time I reached one in my career, in life it felt
hollow.
And the *raasta*? I thought it would teach me something.
But all I found was silence, pain, and breathlessness.
Like cycling from Gurgaon to India Gate, like climbing the
ladder at work.
No matter how far I went, this *bechain dil* always brought
me back to the same emptiness.
So I opened Notion, and wrote with a pen that has no ink
a *besyahi kalam* yet somehow, the page bled anyway.

Rasta

Raste mein kuch mila nahi,
Manzil pe kuch bacha nahi,
Yeh besyahi kalam se apne armaan likh raha hoon...
Maloom nahi isse kuch hoga bhi ya nahi...

Why I wrote this poem

It was usual late Friday night after a fight with my wife.
She had gone to bed, but I couldn't.
I sat in the other room, heart racing, smoking cigarette af-
ter cigarette,
fighting with her in my head writing about it in my jour-
nal like I always do.
Blaming her.
Explaining to myself why I was right.
Why I always am.

But somewhere, mid-sentence, something cracked.
A quiet voice whispered *"What if... it's you?"*

And honestly?
I wasn't ready to hear that.
Not fully.
But the thought didn't leave.
It circled me like smoke.

Maybe it was the first time I realised
I might need help.
Not to fix her.
To understand *me.*

This poem came from that edge
the edge between my ego and the truth.

Jaane Du?

Bechain hoon kyun? Pata karoon ya jaane du?
Saans ghoot si rahi hai, koshish karoon ya jaane du?
Samajh mein aane laga hai maamla sirf mere zehan ka hai.
Keh doon sabse? Ya jaane du?
Main samajh ke khud ko laayak, nikaalta raha kami sab mein,
Galti ab maan loon apni? Ya jaane du?
Mera har sach ab jhooth sa lagne laga hai,
Aakhir sach hai kya?
Pata karoon? Ya jaane du?

Why I wrote this Poem

We were at Starbucks in Ambience Mall, Gurgaon
me, my wife, and my son.
I had been on medication for Bipolar 2 for months. She
brought me out because I was feeling restless at home
craving people, craving normalcy.

Just one wish that day:
to feel normal again.

But within minutes, the noise drained me.
And by evening, even that tiny wish felt too heavy to
hold.

This poem came from that surrender.

Shor

Coffee shop ki bheed mein khamoshi dhoondhta hoon,
Akele kamre mein baitha shor dhoondhta hoon.
Kya ghazab hai tanabana chaahton ka,
Dekh kisi ka Insta jhooth, apna sach badalta hoon.
Apna hi sapna bojh sa ho jaata hai shaam aate-aate,
Jise poora karne ko saara din bhatakta hoon.

Why I wrote this Poem

People doubted me
my caliber, my intent, my worth.

At home.
Among friends.
Even in my marriage.

No one said it to my face. But it showed.
In how they looked at me.
Talked around me.
Tolerated me   while I was still building.

And when I finally had something to show
they all smiled a little wider.
Talked a little softer.
Like I had finally become someone *worthy of love*.

But then came the fall.
I lost it all   especially my confidence.
And that's when they reminded me,
what a dollar becomes once it breaks   just cents.

This poem was written not in anger, but in quiet recognition.

Shakhsiyat

jeb ki gehraiyon mein shakhsiyat ka paimana dekha,
Gaddiyon ke wazan pe maine pyaar ka badh jaana dekha.
Kabhi jinhein main dikhai nahi deta tha,
Aaj unki aankhon mein apne liye pyaar dekha.

Why I wrote this Poem

I had just turned 34.
No job. No plan. No certainty.

All the dreams I once spoke of loudly
either broke, faded, or turned into something else.

And when I looked back, I saw a pattern
moments lived without depth.
Work done without commitment.
Love felt without stillness.
Life spent in small pleasures, like borrowed time.

Kha lo, pee lo, chill karo.
That had become the rhythm.
And now... the song felt stupid.

That day, I wasn't angry at the world.
I was just disappointed in myself.

And this poem wrote itself
like a summary I never meant to file.

4 Din

Sunte-samajhte umr nikal gayi,
Yeh meri zindagi chaar din ki yun hi guzar gayi.
Kha-pa-cha ko sach samajh ke maze se jeeta raha,
Saali life 4 Days 3 Nights ke package mein simat gayi.

Why I wrote this Poem

I talked to Allah every day.
Not for things just to feel heard.
I followed what I was taught:
be good, help others, don't expect too much, pray, be
thankful.

And I did.
I chose love over money.
I forgave. I prayed. I stayed kind.

But still, I broke
Still, I ended up here hopeless, depressed, wanting to
disappear.

I didn't ask for paradise.
Just to be someone's first choice.
To be seen, held, chosen and out of misery

That day, I wasn't praying.
I was asking:
**"Is this faith or was I just talking to a rumour all this
time?"**

Khwaab

Yeh to nahin hona tha, yahi se nikalne ki to dua maangi
thi,
Na mahal maanga tha,
Na shohrat ki chahat thi,
Na Khuda maanga tha,
na qaynaat maangi thi.
Lamahaaton ki khushi maangi,
kya zyadti thi ye bhi?
Khuda, tu hai bhi sach mein,
ya afwaah hai ye bhi,
Aaj kyun khaali haath khada hoon
Is ranj-o-gham ki baarish mein,
Tu hai to sabit kar,
maine to…
har roz tere sajde mein gardan jhuka li thi

Why I wrote this Poem

I wrote this with a heavy heart,
not just for myself, but for my nephew too.

He's a self-aware boy, burdened too early.
Expected to carry everyone's emotions, but never truly
seen.

And when I looked at him, I saw my younger self.
The guilt we inherit.
The roles we never chose.
The way adults break us,
then apologise, expecting peace as if it's owed.

We forgive.
Not because we heal.
But because they need it to die in peace.

But what about us?

After I was diagnosed with Bipolar II,
those questions got louder.
The spirals. The silence. The weight.

And I started to blame.
Not just life.
But the ones who gave it to me.

This poem came from that ache,
the ache of being born without being asked,
and burdened for it ever since.

Duniya, Wazīfe Aur Main

Yeh duniya ke wazīfe aise kyun hain?
Jab itne dukh seh ke bada karna pada humein,
To paida karte kyun hain?
Aur agar kar hi liya, to ehsaan jatana kaisa?
Kya main apni marzi se aaya tha,
ya maine aapko chuna tha?
Darte kaise nahin,
yeh sikhao zara,
Behte aansu rokun kaise,
mujhe batao zara.
Kyun apni kamiyaan mujhpe thopi ja rahi hain,
Apni luti khwahishein mujhse kyun poori karwayi ja rahi
hain?

Why I wrote this Poem

This poem holds three people:
My father. Myself. And now, my son.

When I think of my father, I remember his smell on the
pillow
but not his smile.
Only his stress. His silence. His refusals.
I used to think: maybe it was the rent... maybe money
swallowed his joy.

Then came my turn.
New cities, new homes, constant noise, people talking *at*
each other never *to*.
I never felt I belonged anywhere.
So I turned inward. Solitude became my address.

And now, I have a son.
And with him came a new ache
to break the chain.

To be the home I never had.
To not pass down the silence I inherited.

This poem isn't about flats or money.
It's about three men who lived in houses...
but never felt at home.

Kirayedar

Zindagi kirayedar ki safar si lagti hai,
Na lautne ko ghar, na pahochne ko manzil dikhti hai.
Mahina badalta hain, kiraaya bharte hai,
Zara jo zar joda hai, waqt aane pe todte hai.
Khwahish, zarurat aur madad ka faasle mit'ta jaata hai,
Jitna bhi kar lo, poora nahi pad pata hai.
Bas yahi afsos kirayedar ka,
Ke kaash mera bhi ek ghar hota...
Alishaan na sahi, 10 by 10 ka kamra hota.
Yahi kashmakash mein umr nikal gayi,
Apna ghar hone ki chaah toot ke ab chid si ban gayi.
Khaali kar ye kiraaye ka makaan, laut jaane ko dil karta
hai,
Phir yaad aaya, na gaon hai apna, na door ghar hai koi.
Har teen saal mein makaan badal liye,
Kabhi dost, kabhi school, kabhi khud badal liye.
Kiraaya badhega ye soch ke ghamzada ho lete the,
Naya saal aane ki khushi bas char din mein kho dete the.
Kiraaya badhega to kuch to kam karna hai,
Ab kis apne ka dil tode, ye intezaam karna hai.
Is baar phir bete ko daant ke mana karun,
Ya agle saal ka bahaana daal doon?
Pichhle saal jo taala tha tujhe,
Is saal bhi kaise taal doon?

Why I wrote this Poem

I've lived in toxic patterns.
Or maybe... that's just how a bipolar mind lives.
I have theories. None of them comfort me.

For years, I saw people as liars.
Actors.
Because I couldn't believe kindness could be real, not af-
ter what I lived through.

There was one family.
They took me in like their own.
Helped me grow. Showed me love.
And then one day,
they left me with pain I still don't have words for.

They said I didn't deserve good things.
They called me a parasite.
They said I didn't belong in their home.

And maybe they were right.
But I never used them.
I just returned... when I was broken.
Because I believed that was my home.

This poem came from that wound,
where love and cruelty started looking the same.

Mera Yaar

Woh resha-resha udhed ke mera, mujhe saza deta hai,
Lafzon ke kode barsa ke, mujhe ghutnon pe gira deta hai.
Zulm ki inteha to dekho,
Zillat ke zakhmon pe dhuen ka Malham jab malta hu,
Aake zakhmo ko, naakhun se kured deta hai.

Why I wrote this Poem

25th September. 8:30 PM.
I was standing on a chair in my café.
My laptop charger wrapped around my neck.
The other end knotted to the fan.

I wasn't angry.
I wasn't even sad.
I was done.

Whatever was left of my soul had gone quiet.
Not the kind of quiet that screams.
The kind that simply… lets go.

I wasn't writing a note.
I wasn't making a statement.
I just didn't want to stay.

And then, in that silence,
a memory broke through.
Not a prayer. Not a quote.
Just a voice.

My son's.
"Daddy… aap ghar kab aaoge?"

He wasn't asking for a hero.
He was just waiting for me to come home.
Like he always did.

That moment didn't save me.
It paused me.
And in that pause, I stepped down.

This poem came after.
Not in survival,
but in the ruins of almost not surviving.

For one voice.
For one child.
Who still doesn't know he saved me.

Main Mar Gaya

Aur phir ek din main mar gaya.
Zara si hi to daud lagayi thi umr ki, aur ab main thak
gaya.
samajhna baaki tha khud ko abhi, par ab bhot ho gaya
Aur phir ek din main mar gaya.
Apne ehsaan meri galti ginayi har roz tumne
meri kamio ki list banayi roz tumne
Tumsa bante-bante, main apne aap se dar gaya.
Aur phir ek din main mar gaya.
chalu apni raah pe ya sunu tumhaari,
Bas isi kashmakash mein reh gaya,
Aur phir ek din main mar gaya.

Closing Note

Thank you for reading.
If this book made you feel something you couldn't say out
loud,
I'd love to hear from you.

You can write to me:
✉ **yeahitsmerizwan@gmail.com**
or find me on Instagram:
📷 **@besyahi_kalam**

If you're holding pain, confusion, or questions—I see you.
This book was never meant to heal. But maybe it helped
you feel less alone.

Volume Two is coming.
It begins where this one almost ended.

— Rizwan

www.ingramcontent.com/pod-product-compliance
Lightning Source LLC
Chambersburg PA
CBHW031256130726

47988CB00008B/3381